Mutterings of an Unsettled Mind

Poems by:

Dan Fitzgerald

Mutterings of an Unsettled Mind
©Dan Fitzgerald 2025

All rights reserved. Blue Jade Press, LLC retains the right to reprint this book. Permission to reprint poems from this collection must be obtained by the author.

ISBN- 978-1-961043-16-9

Published by:

Blue Jade Press, LLC

Blue Jade Press, LLC
Vineland, NJ 08360
www.bluejadepress.com

For Louie and Mic

Table of Contents

Unsettled	1
Gift of Night	2
Secret	3
If Blindness Struck	4
Fall in a Jar	5
Pantomime	6
Hard Truth	7
What I Know	8
Contemplation: The World Outside	9
Through the Words	10
When I Was Young	11
Monday, December 10, 2012	12
The Chill Crosses	13
Take Me Away	14
No Longer There	15
A Little Time Passes	16
Falling Away in a Wind	17
Fall	18
A Little Night Music	19
Blue Sky on Tuesday Morning	20
Can I Hear Me Now?	21
Dark Night	22
Ode to Joey	23
Blank Pages	24
Odd Life	25
Heading for the River	26
Hoping For the Best	27
Color in the Sky	28
Enough for Today	29
Darkness Walks	30
Listening to Old Records	31
Shadows Do Not Wait	32
Snow has Fallen	33
Wrong Clock	34

Waiting for a Beginning	35
Memory Landfill	36
December, Not May	37
Fire Storm	38
Good Beginning	39
Another Time	40
I Am Here	41
Far From Me	42
Fantasy	43
If It Had Been Enough	44
Keeping the Battery Charged	45
Keep Sake	46
Around the House	47
Thanksgiving Day 2022	48
Death of a Friend	49
Pass By, Please	50
Winter Afternoon	51
Together	52
Grey Asks For Forgiveness	53
Happy Times	54
Captured	55
Courage	56
February 21	57
Friday 2pm	58
Gift Exchange	59
Good Conversations	60
Hard of Hearing	61
Land of Echoes	62
The Way It Has Always Been	63
The Pen Starts	64
Other Days	65

Unsettled

I have sat in this chair
a long time,
sometimes with music playing,
sometimes in silence;
always watching alone
        the world outside.
Seasons have passed;
my face has grown wrinkled.
The room around me
has become my comfort,
          my refuge,
          my place to
let my mind do its wanderings:
traveling, visiting, exploring
all the places I have been afraid
        to go.
Over the years it has thought
so many things
but it has never found a way
of settling down.

Gift of Night

Mist of morning
leaves with the rising sun,
a gift of the night
       saying goodbye.

Secret

I have lost the day
to the mindless duties
once thought as important,
wasting moments lasting for hours.
Too many of those, I tell myself,
trying to remember the pauses
of taking a breath to follow a cloud
or to look at a bird building a nest.
That is the secret, I think now,
I must use the time I have
not worrying what others are suggesting
but finding all the bits and pieces I need
to make a life I can live in
        with love.

If Blindness Struck

If blindness struck,
my eyes gone dark,
the world would freeze
in my last seeing.
Every person I saw before
would never change,
their best, their worst,
the in between of that day.
A dead branch in a tree
would never fall,
the blooms of flowers
never fade

Litter on roads
would never move;
the color of the sky
forever frozen in its weather.
Voices would become more familiar,
sounds, all the more sweet.
Smells would be the brushes
painting my memories.
The slightest touch would shift my direction.
So much lost, maybe something gained.
The hardest part, never being able to look
into your eyes again.

Fall In a Jar

I wish I could capture
the sun in Fall,
that last warmth
      of a long summer,
storing it away in jars
      large and small.
Then when winter comes,
diminishing the days to cold and grey,
I could go into my stores
      of light and heat,
bringing one out every day.
I would set it on a table
letting the glow of leaves
      light the darkness
and the heat of the glass
      warm the air,
denying that winter will ever last.

Pantomime

It is all pantomime,
this ritual of getting
      through a day.
So much is just motion,
a pretension of action repeating
itself to make it through the hours.
No one suspects this shifting
in the sun's shining is just a ruse.
They do not see the nights
when the make-up is taken off;
the costumes are back in their closets.
No one sees the real face,
the clothes I want to wear,
hiding behind the closed doors.
I am afraid to show anyone those.
So I pretend for another day,
wondering through the darkness
      of the night
if I will ever be able
to be the real me.

Hard Truth

I cannot write like the poets of old
with their words singing, spinning,
stinging across the pages.
I can only write simple words
on simple paper with a
simple pen full of ink.
And when I am done,
I lay the pen on my desk,
to wander to an outside window,
thinking of what I had just written.
I pray that what was revealed
is somehow true.

What I Know

I used to know
all the trees' names:
the oaks, the maples,
elms and sycamores.
I used to know
all the names of the flowers:
roses, lilies, daisies.
I used to know
the planets, the constellations,
the names of stars, the bright and the dim,
the Orion's, guiding Polaris.
I used to know
which birds passed by my window,
flew to a branch, sang in a bush:
a lark, a robin, the red cardinal.
But, that time has passed,
my mind now numb and forgetting.
Yet I still see green all around,
all the colors in bloom,
The sun shines its light.
The birds sing and fly.
There is so much I no longer know
but what I do recognize
is so important to me now.

Contemplation: The World Outside

The world outside goes about its business,
filling the hours of the day,
waiting for dark so it may rest.

I watch from my window.
What is the hurry?
The sun is shining,
birds are enjoying wind and sky.
There is so much that can wait.
Why ruin such a pretty day?

It is nice to have such luxury,
to not worry about tomorrow,
just to take the day as it goes,
always finding something new.

When darkness finds its way to me,
as it always must,
I will not completely rest
but I will be content that my day
was not full of hurry and busy,
but was filled, at least,
with some contemplations.

Through the Words

It is hard to read
through these words
reimagining why they were written
and what they mean now.
Some seem so important,
they needed to be said.
Others just sit on the page
like children caught at school,
sent out into the hall
to await their fate.
Most mystify me,
wondering how they came to be,
where they came from,
scaring me at times
of the emotions that released them,
and why those same emotions
have somehow now
        gone away.

When I Was Young

When I was young,
the world was old
but not to me.
It was new and fresh,
needing to be seen
for the first time.
Now as the years catch up to me,
I have grown from boy to man,
seeing the world differently.
There is no age that matters to it.
It has always been here,
watching me grow.
My days are just passing clouds
in its forever sky.
And when I am gone
      it will not be old
      or young,
except to those
      who know it after me.

Monday, December 10, 2012

I wonder why I write the date
on some of these pages.
It isn't like this day is so important.
Maybe if I die that day,
people will come across these words
       and say
"Gosh, isn't that interesting
what he wrote just before he went."
Not really.
They are just ordinary words
written on a particular day,
trying to seem more
important
       with a date.

The Chill Crosses

The chill crosses into me,
a shiver of fear
flashing like lightning
      before a storm at night.
I shake, shuddering, waiting
for the coming thunder.
And when it comes,
      I weep inside
not knowing how strong
the tempest will be.
But I must wait in darkness
hoping that the next flash
will bring a semblance of heat
to drive the coldness out of me.

Take Me Away

Take me away from here,
this place of angry words
and disturbed faces.
Take me to a sea
with knowing waves
laughing with the sand,
to dapple shaded woods
with tamped down heat passing
in transient breezes.
I want to hear the birds,
the rustling of leaves,
the laughter of children
touching water for the first time.
Guide me away from this place
with its shrill singing
of discordant melodies.
I want to hear the songs
of the universe, its stars' voices
harmonizing to the beating
of my heart.

No Longer There

I am waiting.
It won't be long.
I can feel the beginnings
as the world around me recedes.
Oh, I hear it,
      see it,
even pretend I am in it.
But I am losing the feeling
          for it
and soon, it will not matter.
An hour, maybe longer,
that is usually how long it takes
until the body goes numb,
pain descends to memory
and I relax in false comfort.
Slowly then, the mind drifts,
not caring what it knows,
just watching the world go past.
Relief is the promise.
A relief of wanting, a limpness
not of me, because
I am no longer there.

A Little Time Passes

We give the day its due
with its sun or clouds,
rain or clear sky.
Counting them too fast,
we constantly wish for more.
But when night descends
with its shrouding veil,
we call the day what it is,
then go home to rest,
not thinking it may have been our last.
The next morning we wake,
not wondering how many more.
We go about our tasks,
using the hours in our own way,
never thinking to stop and watch our world,
to let a little time go past.

Falling Away in a Wind

It is confusing inside my head;
can't seem to find any kind of focus.
Thoughts drift around,
landing like a leaf hitting a window,
then falling away in a wind.
That is nice, sometime, this listening,
waiting, curious to see what will
come across the glass. As the window grows dark
and another day fades to grey,
I wonder if perhaps it is time to grab one of those leaves
and follow the wind that carries it away.

Fall

Twilight chases bright sun
shining in a blue sky;
the chill of night not far behind.
Rust colored leaves cling tenuously,
lingering in the skeletal
outlines of trees, dropping, releasing
themselves into a fickle wind,
landing them into the last shadows
of a past time summer.
They creep across unfamiliar ground,
searching, finally coming to rest, unmoving,
except by passing foot, hungry bird,
a wind pushing an unseen quest.
Accepting the loss of a high flying life,
past the limit of a cold sky, geese gather
to head for warmer, calmer climes.

A Little Night Music

Songs are heard
as day finishes its work,
night begins its duties.
The notes float in the air,
hovering in the shadows
of a setting sun.
Unafraid of the coming dark,
music fills the sky with stars.

Blue Sky on Tuesday Morning

Friends call now and then,
not as many as years ago.
Some have died, some moved away,
some never bother anymore.
You know how it is.
Called one the other day,
talked like time had never passed.
Both knew that was a lie,
just like our promise of doing this more often.
The phone went quiet in my hand,
staring silently eyeless
until dark, saving itself
for some other time.

Can I Hear Me Now?

I live in silence
        afraid to speak
any words that someone else
        might hear.
In the quiet of my
        not speaking,
others listen to words
        but none are my own.
No one hears the sentences
I pronounce in my head,
condemning me to a cell
        of isolation.
Surrounded by walls of not speaking,
I can find uncritical peace,
unashamed of the naked words
        I can think but
                not share.
It is there I listen loudest
        to the echoes of a universe
                captured in my soul.

Dark Night

Time has stopped,
pausing to take a breath,
to let a moment pass
without the need to mark its journey.
What a miracle that would be
to stop all clocks,
       the motion of stars,
to be completely still, without worry
of what it has cost
in our haste for an ending.
For one second; an hour;
maybe even a century,
all gone without consequence.
Just to be in a universe,
no longer held hostage
       to a future or a past,
with no need for memory.
Perhaps that is what happens
       in death.

Ode to Joey

The day is nearly over,
        a day's light grows long.
Outside a soon to be closed window,
        a high school band plays
               a song.
A neighbor mows a lawn,
        a car is being washed,
one bloom remains on a rose bush.
        The band plays on.
There was a girl
        who liked that tune.
There was a day
        longer than today.
That was a time
        when the world was new.
Those are yesterday's smiling now
as the sun folds its light.

Blank Pages

They ask quiet questions,
those voices from the heart.
Does tomorrow really matter
if today is left alone?
Will the sun really shine,
if all is hiding behind clouds?
How can eyes be so blue,
when their color is soft brown?

Couples walk hand in hand,
their steps matching a forward march.
Graves side by side, united by a single stone.
A message in a bottle
lasts forever if never found.
You were with me yesterday,
here is a picture for a reminder.
There is no response
to these queries from the heart,
just blank pages
where the answers were
supposed to be.

Odd Life

My mind is full of the random
        and the strange.
A remark made to me in third grade,
the first two lines of a hundred songs;
some face I had known
        but can't find a name,
memories from somewhere
        that may or may not be true.
If this is my life flashing before me as I die,
my final thoughts will have to be:
my what an odd time you have had.

Heading For the River

I can hear the geese calling
in the cold winter air,
their voices singing in the wind,
disturbing the still clinging leaves
of almost barren trees.

Their wings are silent here
      in my enclosed little room,
yet I remember the effortless whoosh
of their flying as I stood in summer sun
watching them pass over my head.

They are heading for open water
as they cross over my frozen pond.
Probably the river below the dam.
remembering the last gathering I saw.
Not far to them but what is distance
for those who use the sky for a highway.

Hoping For the Best

I gave blood today,
a relatively painless way
to make a difference in someone's life.

That person may be a complete stranger
with nothing in common with me,
other than the type of blood in our veins.
But who am I to judge?

They may go on to sire generations
of cancer-curing, world-feeding,
Mid-East-peace-solving,
richer than dirt philanthropists.

Or maybe —
they will raise a race of Hitler's, Stalin's
an Anti-Christ or two,
destroying all civilization as we know it.

Hey that's life —
you give a little of yourself,
hoping it will be for the best,
that it will all work out.
You never really know, though,
at least you tried.

Color In the Sky

I am not ready to go back
to all the words that I have written.
I leave them alone for a time,
then touch them once more
to see if they still touch me.
But not today,
the rain is too cold,
the trees still hold their leaves,
afraid, like me, to let them go.
This day is grey,
with color washed away.
Not a good day, I feel,
to revisit words written in the dark,
or even those shining in the sun.
Better to wait for a time
when there is color in the sky.

Enough for Today

The burnt-orange sun fights
the grey smoke of clouds.
Garbage cans wait on the street,
lonely soldiers ready
to be hollowed out by fate.
A small heater warms the room.
I can hear the electric meter spinning.
That's next month's problem.
There is enough already for today.

Darkness Walks

Quiet night, silent night;
darkness walks without a sound.

Listening to Old Records

Staring at the floor vent
near the stereo,
words and music scratch
through the seldom used speakers.
Vinyl crackles around the room.
I sit with the album covers
spread out before me,
listening like these sounds were new
and the memories that go with them
were things yet to happen.

Shadows Do Not Wait

Shadows do not wait
for night to come
to claim their share
      of the dark.
The paths they take
lead them to any light
they may need,
      stealing reflections
from all who cross their wanderings.
And when night has reached
its blackest midnight,
they lurk patiently, eager
to pursue any shining
that may shape their
shifting wiliness.

Snow Has Fallen

Snow has fallen
crisp and deep.
I watched it all night
unable to sleep.
Now that it is day
with light enough to see,
I am staying home
and watch TV.

Wrong Clock

Licked the spoon
from a dirty ice cream bowl.
Called the moon
a nasty name before it set.
Couldn't wait
for the day to be over.
Saw two girls
walking down a street;
neither cared
if they were lost.
This is the way it has to be,
watching time pass
on someone else's clock.

Waiting for a Beginning

Dark starts earlier these days.
The sun seems worn down
from its summer job of shining.

Leaves are losing their green,
changing to orange and yellow,
sometimes red.

My evening walks are guarded
by street lights now,
chased by shadows.

Some people like this time of year,
with its crisp air, no mowing of grass.
I enjoy it, though today's coming winter
bothers more than yesterday's spring.

I miss the growing things,
the newness of the earth.
All life must pause to start again.
But the older I get,
the longer it takes for me
to wait for the beginnings.

Memory Landfill

Take a picture
of all of us together,
friend or foe,
brother and sister,
      lovers and haters,
all here.

Put it in an album,
frame it for a wall,
hide it in a drawer
away from the sun to fade.

Someday it will not matter
where it has been kept,
a family reunion collection maybe
or perhaps sold in an antique mall.

Most likely, though, it will end
as a scrap blowing
      down a lost highway,
escaped from a memory landfill
built by us all.

December, Not May

November feels like May.
Here inside it is already winter
with no hope of an early spring.
Don't be so negative, my friends say,
but I know these warm days
cool nights, cannot last.
Bitter cold, deepening snow
are still in the forecast.
I try to enjoy this time
like a wish on a star
that may come true.
But too many stars have fallen
in my empty sky
and the calendar paces off November
toward the beginning of December
not May.

Fire Storm

The mist and haze has found us
hiding in our havens, thinking
we are safe from harm.
As the sky grows weary
in fighting for blue,
the sun dims in sadness.
Clouds are hidden in the daze
of smoke from far off fires.
We go about our business,
pretending it is all normal,
but our hearts beat faster
fearing the poor earth
is fighting for its life,
and for ours.

Good Beginning

The morning brings the end
to night's cool air.
Leaves change color to begin the fall.
A high school band warms up
before classes begin.
Back-packed children play
as they go down the street.
A bird hurries inside
a dirty-white house
hanging from a tree.
There is an unopened letter
on the dining room table.
A woman sweeps her steps.
It is a new day, and nowhere
is the sound of war.

Another Time

There was a time
when I would sit in the evening
watching shadows wash their hands
 in the dark, leaving the night
         clean of the day.
Some whiskey would wait
in a half-empty glass.
A hint of music would play
somewhere in the air.
My mind would clear itself,
         like the shadows,
of any doubts left by the suns
         last shining.

Now I watch clouds
take over the sky
as the shadows now hurry
to uncleaned corners.
No glass stands ready for solace.
The rooms around are all silent
and doubts linger, like the memory
of a day that never truly went away.

I Am Here

There is an owl in the night.
I can hear its call in the dark,
sporadic, specific, sounding
like a plea.
Or perhaps, just a voice
among the stars, telling
anyone who will listen
I am here.

Far From Me

Snow gathers in the trees,
falling to cover the grass.
A wind moves through branches;
a mailman short-cuts his route

I heard her voice
on a message left on a phone.
It sounded like it was yesterday,
it was so far from me.

The street is empty of traffic.
A house has a light shining above its door.
No one is there knocking,
no one is asking to be let in.

There is a picture of her in the paper.
A story tells how great she had been.
I wish she was here now
but she is so far from me now
to ever come back home.

Fantasy

I am tired of the world
        this day
with its wars and turmoil,
always seeming to destroy
all that was given to us
as a gift to enjoy.

I see the wonders of the sky
and earth starting each day
as if it were new.
I watch people trying to
get through their days
with joy and kindness and mercy.
But somehow the violence
the cruelty, the storms
always occur.

It is the way it is,
        I am told
You have to understand.

        Not today.

Today I am going to
do something else.
I am going to think of other
ways of life,
of other outcomes.
Then perhaps then
I will be at peace.

If It Had Been Enough

Night has come.
I am writing words on paper
lit only by a small lamp,
as the world outside
hides in dark.
It is okay,
        I do this a lot.
Probably why my words
are so faint.
I wish I was more tired;
I would be in bed,
reading until sleep.
But here I sit,
        pen in hand,
wondering if this is
all that will make the page.
It is like so much I do,
a wan effort
        to get through a day.
In that time before
I finally turn out the light,
I sit staring into the night,
thinking of what I had done,
hoping it had been enough.

Keeping the Battery Charged

The phone lays quiet and still,
a useless tool now.
No vibration, no unique song,
no bell or ding or any sonic nudge.
Time passes in all the usual ways
but all the while anticipating
an interruption, signaling
that somewhere, something or someone
wants to hear a voice or accept
the touch of a finger on a pad.
Hopefully it is a real human being
trying to communicate that
in all the universe, I am still wanted.

Keep Sake

I remember a white house
      by a river,
with me resting on a couch,
listening to the rain hitting
a tin roof, frightened
by a storm that made
the windows explode
      in light and sound.

It is only a memory
      of childhood.
Like so many, a snapshot
of long ago, now seen
      with older eyes.

Then it fades into a today,
no longer seeming important,
but it must have been.
That is why I still keep it.

Around the House

I walk around the house
tallying all that is here,
wandering, wondering:
      Why is that picture crooked?
      How long has that been there?
      Why does everything get so dusty,
when no one comes or goes?
But the dishes are done,
The bed is made.
There is a clean window
to look out at the day.
Someday, someone will find me here,
alone, looking asleep,
with all these things still here.
      And then
they will wander and wonder
through the rooms:
      Is he really gone?
      What is in that drawer?
      That is a nice photo.
When was it taken?

What do we do with all this now?

Thanksgiving Day 2022

The world is so strange to me,
though it is filled with familiar things.
I wake in the morning, doing
my waking up rituals, settling into my day.
But it all feels so alien.
Maybe the sun has not been up long enough.
Maybe the coffee has not reached my brain.
I watch the sky and clouds pass.
I feel like I am still in a dream from sleep.
What has happened during the night
to make all this so?
I have heard no news,
do not know any forecast.
Everything is in its place,
but touched somehow by time.

Death of a Friend

Night shrouds fearful moonlight.
Stars stare out of the darkness.
No twinkling, no sparkling,
no shimmering flirtations
with passing clouds.
Only saddened light dripping blackness,
passing trains sounding, moaning,
then hurrying into an echo.
An airplane disappears in a fading trail.
A child cries without warning,
quickly hushed into silence.
Birds fly mutely into trees.
Headlights fade on a passing street.

Pass By, Please

Walk on past
to other windows.
You've seen me
in this one before.

Winter Afternoon

A sun brightens the frozen snow.
Clouds have run with the wind,
seeking more inviting climes.
On the hard crust of white,
there are no foot prints;
the passing of friends and strangers
rejected by the harsh cold's shell.
A small bird huddles in a bush,
feathers puffed to a coat of warmth.
It stares at the cruel ground,
looking for a morsel to steal.
It knows its serendipitous theft
will go unnoticed, with no tracks
showing on the unmarked earth.

Together

We are together in the dark,
letting the corruption
of our bodies
dissolve together.
No matter to us,
used to our couplings.
It is here, though,
in our graves,
that we depart from ourselves,
becoming not two bodies,
but one spirit.

Grey Asks For Forgiveness

A bird flies
across a sky:
clouds follow.

A word speaks,
silent sound
echoes near.

Grey asks for forgiveness.

Happy Times

I wish it would rain,
hiding the sun in dark grey.
No birds in the air,
no rays of light,
just flashes of lightning
to show the sky is still there.
These days are too bright,
the sky too blue.
Flowers are glowing
in new found colors;
so proud, so pleased.
I need to see the gloom,
to feel the sorrow of the earth.
It is time for night to begin,
to drive away the happy day.

Captured

She stands by her easel,
her eyes scanning the figure of me
sitting on the shore of a pond.
Her hands move over the canvas.
I am watching the light on water,
my hand poised with camera.
Seeing her with her palette,
she becomes part of my vision.
I take a picture; she slashes a couple of strokes.
She is now frozen in my camera's memory
and I in her brush and paint.
Both of us are now waiting to see
if what we have captured
will be important enough to save.

Courage

Your eyes hide the telling
of roads taken and abandoned,
memories searching deep in vision.
Paths can be followed, though,
in the creases wandering
around the bright colors
dancing in your smile.
Tell me, someday if you wish,
about all your journeys
and how they were taken.
Maybe then, I will get the courage
to tell of my own.

February 21

I sat in my chair last night
listening to the furnace air
exhale through the room.
I was thinking of people I once knew.
A clock sounded in the kitchen,
its hands slowly waving
good bye to the time.
I stared at the ceiling
as it stared back.
I wondered about all those people I knew,
how we came into each other's lives.
It is a mystery how that happens
but happens it does.
It really didn't help though,
in a night, sitting in a chair, alone.

Friday 2pm

Sun cast shadows
sneak across the snow.
A birdhouse sways empty
in an afternoon breeze.
On the hour, a clock chimes a call,
another answers down the hall.
The street is deserted, yards are lonely,
      the phone lies silent.
Staring out a window,
I listen for a voice,
one I heard before.
"Not anymore," I hear myself whisper,
turning away from the glass.

Gift Exchange

Yesterday was like any day,
except now it has passed
into memory.
Remembered now more as a relic
than as a gift.

Good Conversations

I have conversations
with all the people around me
when they are no longer there.
We talk of the problems of the world,
solving every one.
Then we decide how to fix the future
so conflict never happens again.
I have to admit
that these conversations
are somewhat one-sided,
but I am pleased
that they all end
with everyone agreeing with me.

Hard Of Hearing

It is hard to speak into silence.
Its echoes leave little room
for words to be heard.

Land of Echoes

I live in a land of echoes,
subtle and loud reverberations
shuddering through me.
I catch them in dreams
and in passing winds;
so familiar, so far away,
so close, I feel them in my heart.
Many are from so long ago,
they are ancient memories
whose meanings are hidden
by too many pasts.
Others are yesterday,
a repeating of experience
trying for another chance in today.
Sometimes, though, they are from tomorrow,
the future looking to correct failures yet to come.
I do not listen to them anymore.
I just feel their vibrations,
always leaving me in wonder.

The Way It Has Always Been

I have no yesterday
for they are still my todays.
All the voices I can hear,
all the faces, have never changed.
The clock has stopped
      in my poor mind,
just ticking the same moment
        over and over
          with no need for tomorrow,
        or anything like a past.
In my small world now,
nothing moves on.
The good times, the bad times,
the memories we are to share
are just what I have now.
I am living them every day.
I do not understand the calendars
      around me.
I can not find the pages
      from long ago.
It is me here, the way I have always been.
No regrets, no wishing for what
could have been different.
It is all occurring now,
the way it has always been.

The Pen Starts

The pen hesitates,
then starts across the page-
words, sentences, vowels and consonants.
The hand moves the pen,
the pen inks the paper.
Staggering, rapidly writing the lines,
I write, detached, aloof, possessed.
Until it all stops without a sigh.

I read the words later:
a week, a month, a year.
"Where did that come from," I wonder.
It is my handwriting, but
it has been hijacked.
It looks like something written by me
but not me; some secret-self hiding in me
        now revealed.

Other Days

My mind wanders back
to other days, other times,
taking my heart with it.
Was that only yesterday
that the sun was so bright?
Is there still time to find
a sky unmoved by dark clouds?
No matter now, I think,
looking at all I have around me.
This is the time I have,
given to me by all
that came before.
It is here to be enjoyed,
to hold onto for a little while.
My mind smiles at the memories,
my heart aches for what was lost.
Oh, yes, they agree, but look
at all you have found.

Dan Fitzgerald is an award winning poet and two time Pushcart Award nominee. His work has appeared in *The Writer's Journal, Blindman's Rainbow, Origami Press, Nomad's Choir* and many others. His work has also been included in many anthologies. He is the author of a two collections of poetry, "Weatherman" and "Gatherings" (Kelsay Press) He lives quietly in Pontiac, Illinois tending to home and garden.

www.ingramcontent.com/pod-product-compliance
Lightning Source LLC
Chambersburg PA
CBHW051707090426
42736CB00013B/2576